Things That
Make You Go
YUCK!

Head louse

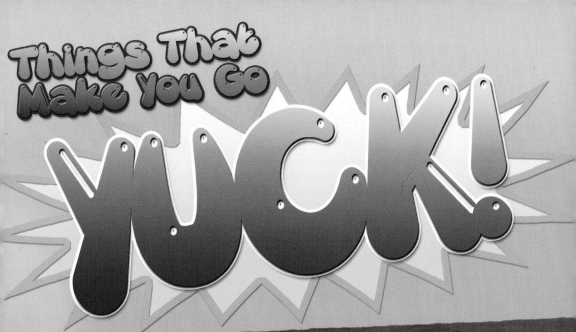

# Things That Make You Go

# YUCK!

## Mystifying Mutants

Jenn Dlugos & Charlie Hatton

Prufrock Press Inc.
Waco, Texas

Library of Congress Cataloging-in-Publication Data

Names: Dlugos, Jenn, author. | Hatton, Charlie, author.
Title: Things that make you go yuck! : mystifying mutants/by Jenn Dlugos
  and Charlie Hatton.
Other titles: Mystifying mutants
Description: Waco, Texas : Prufrock Press Inc., [2017] | Audience: Ages 9-12.
  | Includes bibliographical references.
Identifiers: LCCN 2016035485 | ISBN 9781618215642 (pbk.)
Subjects: LCSH: Animal mutation--Juvenile literature. | Mutation
  (Biology)--Juvenile literature. | Animals--Abnormalities--Juvenile
  literature. | Variation (Biology)--Juvenile literature. |
  Genetics--Juvenile literature.
Classification: LCC QH390 .D5845 2017 | DDC 576.5/49--dc23
LC record available at https://lccn.loc.gov/2016035485

Copyright © 2017, Prufrock Press Inc.
Edited by Lacy Compton
Cover and layout design by Raquel Trevino

ISBN-13: 978-1-61821-564-2

Printed in the United States of America.

At the time of this book's publication, all facts and figures cited
are the most current available. The author and Prufrock Press Inc.
make no warranty or guarantee concerning the information and
materials given out by organizations or content found at websites,
and we are not responsible for any changes that occur after this book's
publication. If you find an error, please contact Prufrock Press Inc.

Prufrock Press Inc.
P.O. Box 8813
Waco, TX 76714-8813
Phone: (800) 998-2208
Fax: (800) 240-0333
http://www.prufrock.com

Albino hedgehog

# Table
## of Contents

# Introduction

## Mutants.

The word doesn't exactly fill you with a warm fuzzy feeling, does it? Maybe it reminds you of half-animal superhumans wreaking havoc on a city. Or man-eating insects crawling through town. Or your siblings when they wake up in the morning. In reality, mutants are not just gross critters that pop out of a science-fiction story (or the next bedroom). Real-life mutants walk, slither, and creep among us, all due to some horked-up genes.

## Genes: Your Personal Operating System

Just like your computer, your body comes preprogrammed. Your genes are your internal hard drive. They store all the instructions to make your traits—like hair or eye color—and the necessary programs to build and operate your human body. Your genes carry the blueprints to build the parts that allow you to talk, just like a dog's genes have blueprints to make body parts for barking. (And we're *very* glad those two blueprints never get mixed up. Otherwise, things would get pretty embarrassing when the teacher calls on you in class.)

## Your Code's Written All Over Your Face (And Everywhere Else)

Unlike a computer, your genes are not stored on a central hard drive. They're actually a part of your DNA, which is stored in the nucleus of your cells. (And you have a *lot* of those—you are a living, walking machine of about 37 trillion cells.) All the DNA in one of your cells—including genes and nongene regions—is called your genome. Genes are simply sections of DNA that code for a particular trait or characteristic.

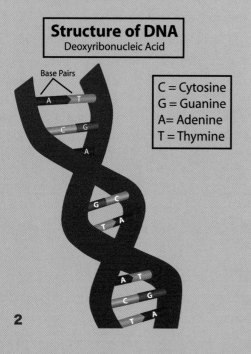

**Structure of DNA**
Deoxyribonucleic Acid

Base Pairs

C = Cytosine
G = Guanine
A = Adenine
T = Thymine

## DN-Eh?

DNA stands for deoxyribonucleic acid (or "DEE-ox-ee-RYE-bow-new-clay-ic" acid, which is quite a mouthful, so it's always just called DNA). It looks a lot like a twisted ladder. The rungs of the ladder are made up of four bases, abbreviated as A, T, C, and G. A pairs with T to form a rung and C pairs with G. Together, these four little letters make up a super-duper long code that turns into you!

## Houston, We Have a Problem

Your DNA tries really hard not to make mistakes in its code, but it isn't perfect. A mutation is any change in the DNA sequence. Sometimes an A accidentally gets paired with a C instead of a T, or a whole section of the code gets deleted. Other times a base squeezes in where it shouldn't be or a whole gene duplicates itself. Mutations can happen due to outside factors—like exposure to harmful chemicals—or when your DNA makes a mistake copying itself when your body makes new cells. Some mutations get passed down from parents to children, and children can pick up new mutations the parents didn't have, too.

## The Biggest Superhero League in the World

If being a mutant was the only criterion for becoming a superhero, then we'd all need to cape up. Every single one of us—including you—has mutations in our DNA, but we don't really notice, because most mutations don't cause a significant change in our traits or body function. But some mutations can really muck things up, genetically speaking, and create some really interesting critters. Many of these outrageous oddities are lurking for you inside this book. Turn the page, if you dare . . .

Orca whale

# 1 Sea Monsters

**We go to the movies to see fearsome pirates battle giant** Krakens or a super-shark take on a fishing boat, but we can rest easy knowing that these sea mutants came from a dark, slimy cavern in someone's imagination. Or do they? Thankfully, we don't need to worry too much about a Sharknado attacking us, but there are plenty of genetic sea monsters crawling, gliding, and oozing under the water. This chapter showcases some of the wettest and wildest mutants on Earth.

## Do You Know Your Mutants?

In 2011, a one-eyed sea creature was found in Mexico. What was it?

a. An orca whale     b. A hermit crab     c. A dusky shark

Find out the answer at the end of the chapter!

# Henry the Hexapus

There's an old fishing boat saying: Fishing is like a box of chocolates; you never know what you're going to get.

Maybe that's more of a shrimp boat thing. But it's true, as a crew of Welsh lobstermen found out in 2008. Lobsters are caught in "pots," cages with bait inside dropped to the ocean floor. Hungry lobsters climb in, but so can other critters like crabs, scuba divers—and octopi.

("Octopi" is a plural of "octopus." Two other plurals—"octopuses" and "octopodes"—are also acceptable. "Octopusseseses" is not acceptable, apparently. But it is a lot of fun to say.)

6

That lobster boat crew found octopi among their catch that day, but one was odd. It only had six legs. So it wasn't an "octopus" (which means "eight-footed") at all. It was a hexapus.

But this not-octopus wasn't missing limbs from an accident or because he'd left his tentacles in his other octopus pants. He'd simply grown that way. His lack of leggage was likely due to a gene mutation, possibly in a Hox gene. Other oddly-legged octopi have also been seen—some with seven legs (a septopus!), nine legs (nonopus!) or even 10. (Ahoy, decapus!)

Meanwhile, our hexapus had a happy ending. He was sent to a local aquarium, dubbed Henry the Hexapus, and spent his days munching on hermit crabs and stretching his (six) legs. Like they say: Fishing is like a pot of octopi; you never know how many legs you're going to get.

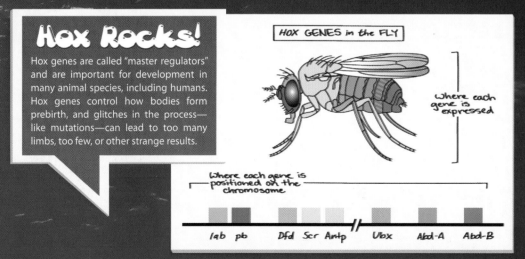

# Hox Rocks!

Hox genes are called "master regulators" and are important for development in many animal species, including humans. Hox genes control how bodies form prebirth, and glitches in the process—like mutations—can lead to too many limbs, too few, or other strange results.

HOX GENES in the FLY

where each gene is expressed

Where each gene is positioned on the chromosome

lab   pb      Dfd  Scr  Antp      Ubx      Abd-A      Abd-B

# The Game of Cones

N ature plays more than its fair share of practical jokes. Take the cone snail, for instance. These colorful, sea-dwelling creatures carry some of the deadliest venom on the planet. Some species carry venom strong enough to kill a human, never mind a tiny sea critter. Yet, the cone snail is also as slow as . . . well, a snail. So, how dangerous can it really be? Any fish worth its sea salt could surely outswim it with one fin tied behind its back, right?

Wrong. The cone snail does have one fast-moving body part—a harpoon-like tooth that injects prey with its deadly venom. (This snail takes the term slow*poke* a bit too literally.) After its feast stops struggling, this cone-shelled assassin slows down to a snail's pace, taking its dear sweet time to swallow its prey whole.

Cone snails' venom is actually one of the most complex venoms in the world, containing more than 100 different neurotoxins (poisons that affect the nerves, brain, and spinal cord). It's so complex that scientists have not been able to make an antivenom for it yet. The genes that make this toxin for the snail are some of the fastest mutating genes in the animal kingdom. Over time the mutations have fine-tuned the toxin, so it can kill or paralyze prey efficiently.

They say bad news travels fast, but apparently not as fast as cone snail mail.

## Sweet and Deadly

There are more than 500 species of cone snail, but only a few are dangerous to humans. Some snails even use a potent form of insulin in their venom. Insulin is a chemical that controls your blood sugar levels. Cone snails use this insulin to send their prey into a deadly sugar crash before they even know what hit them.

# Blinded by

# Fishy Science

They say the eyes are the window to the soul, but what if you don't have any? In freshwater rivers in Mexico lives a little fish known as the Mexican tetra. It has all the standard fishy characteristics—shiny skin, flippy fins, and googly eyes—but don't let its cuteness fool you. This fish has a *lot* of weirdos in its family. Deep below the surface, in the subterranean caves, lives the Mexican cave fish. It's the exact same species as the Mexican tetra, but the cave fish has no eyes.

Granted, there isn't much to see in a pitch-black underwater cave, but wouldn't it be better to have eyes than not? Actually, no. Eyes use energy, so it's actually better for the fish to kick its eyeballs to the curb. Scientists found that the blind cave fish have mutations in about a dozen eye genes that the Mexican tetra do not, but not all blind fish have the same genetic recipe. Fish from different caves can develop different mutations with the same no-eyed result. When scientists mated cave fish from different caves, they produced some offspring with functioning eyes, because the offspring did not inherit the precise combination of mutations to make them blind. Blind cave fish can also mate with the sighted tetra variety and produce sighted offspring. As the old saying goes: An eye for an eye for a . . . fish?

## Visiting the Fish Eye Doctor

As embryos, blind cave fish start to develop eyes, but the eyes degenerate as the fish grow, making them totally blind. A flap of skin grows over the area where functioning eyes should be. Scientists recently found that they can make blind cave fish grow full eyes underneath this skin simply by inserting an eye lens from a sighted tetra fish into a cave fish.

# Ice(fish) Water in Their Veins

B lood, as a rule, is red. That's due to a protein called hemoglobin (he-meh-GLOW-bin), which is red in color and carries oxygen through the blood. Because oxygen is pretty important for our survival, so is hemoglobin. All vertebrates—animals with backbones, including birds, mammals, reptiles, amphibians, and many fish—depend on hemoglobin to transport oxygen.

Except. (In biology, there's always an "except.")

Of about 50,000 known vertebrate species, just one family (16 species total) comes up short on hemoglobin. Known as crocodile icefish, they live in the chilly waters around Antarctica. They were discovered in 1927 by sailors from a Norwegian expedition, who noted the icefish had no scales, big gaping jaws (hence the "crocodile" name), and colorless blood.

Scientists later tested icefish DNA and found that the hemoglobin genes were either missing or mutated beyond repair. Icefish still need oxygen, but without hemoglobin, they can only use the oxygen that dissolves in their blood—10 times less than other vertebrate fish get.

Most animals couldn't survive with these mutations. Luckily for icefish, the cold waters they swim in are rich in oxygen. Still, they have to work a lot harder just to get by. Icefish need 4 times more blood than other fish, and grow bigger hearts and wider blood vessels. Maybe they should invest in some tiny scuba tanks instead!

## How's That Hemoglobin?

Hemoglobin is a protein in blood that carries oxygen from the lungs—or in fish, gills—to the rest of the body for energy. In mammals (like humans), hemoglobin is found in red blood cells and allows blood to carry 70 times more oxygen than could dissolve in blood directly.

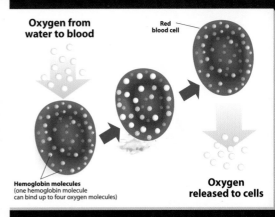

Oxygen from water to blood

Red blood cell

Hemoglobin molecules
(one hemoglobin molecule can bind up to four oxygen molecules)

Oxygen released to cells

# The Lobster Pot at the End of the Rainbow

Whether you drool when you see a big, buttery lobster in a restaurant or you wouldn't touch one with a 10-foot spork, we can all agree that most uncooked lobsters are brown and cooked lobsters are red. If you saw a lobster crawling around a fish market tank that was hot pink or electric blue or neon green, you'd probably complain. (But if it's wearing all of those colors, the lobster may just think it's 1985. Especially if it's sporting a seaweed mullet.)

Both genes and diet affect a lobster's color. Lobsters store a red pigment from plants they eat in their shell. The lobster's body also makes blue and yellow pigments, and the three colors combine to give the lobster an overall brown color. If lobsters do not eat these plants, they will have an all-blue body. Other lobsters are blue due to a gene mutation. These lobsters will stay blue no matter what they eat. A few lobsters lack the proper genes to make the blue and yellow pigments correctly, so they look like a red cooked lobster even when they're alive.

One of the weirdest lobsters lives in the New England Aquarium. His name is Pinchy, and they call him a Halloween lobster, because he's half orange and half brown-black, split right down the middle. We wonder what costume Pinchy wants to wear for Halloween this year, but he probably won't tell us the truth. He's a little two-faced like that.

## Ghost Lobster

The rarest lobster is an albino lobster—only one in 100 million lobsters have this coloration. Albino lobsters do not turn red when you cook them. They'll come out of the pot looking the same color as when they went in—pure white.

# Think About It

Humans have adapted to life on land, but we can also develop new technologies so we can survive in very different environments, like outer space. Pretend you want to build a home to live underwater. What would you need to survive? What would your home look like?

Dusky shark

# Mutant Trivia Answer

In 2011, a one-eyed sea creature was found in Mexico. What was it?

a. An orca whale
b. A hermit crab
c. **A dusky shark (correct)**

It looked like something found in a horror movie, but a dusky shark fetus with one massive eye in the center of its head was found in Mexico. The condition is called *cyclopia* (sigh-CLOE-pee-uh, named after the mythical cyclops), and it is sometimes caused by a mutation that controls the SHH gene, which scientists named after Sonic the Hedgehog.

Long-haired
guinea pig

# 2 Man's Freaky Best Friends

**Most of the mutants in this book are proof that nature** does its best to make sure the wild stays . . . well, wild. But the creepy critters in this chapter are ones that we bring on ourselves. These feathered, finned, and furry mutants may make us go "Eek!", "Whaaaaaat?", or "Yuck!", but they all call our sofas and barns their homes.

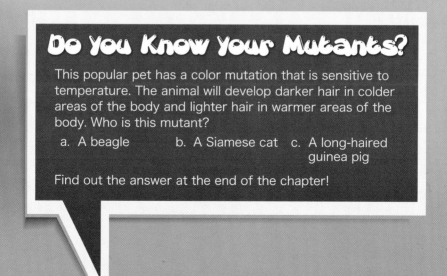

## Do You Know Your Mutants?

This popular pet has a color mutation that is sensitive to temperature. The animal will develop darker hair in colder areas of the body and lighter hair in warmer areas of the body. Who is this mutant?

a. A beagle     b. A Siamese cat     c. A long-haired guinea pig

Find out the answer at the end of the chapter!

# Do You Wanna
# Arowana?

Which is more expensive: an aquarium fish or a new car? Usually, the answer is obvious; a Jaguar costs more than a goldfish, every time. Even if the goldfish has power steering.

But one fish family has something special up its flipper-sleeve. Arowanas (air-oh-WAH-nahs) are freshwater southern-hemisphere fish and popular with folks who keep large fish tanks. The "large" part is important, because aquarium arowanas grow up to 3 feet long. They can also leap 6 feet in the air, live 50 years or more, and come in most every color of the rainbow.

These traits make arowanas popular aquarium fish. But a few very rare arowanas are as valuable as a leather-seated luxury sedan due to a certain kind of mutation. So-called "platinum" arowanas have a genetic condition known as *leucism* (LEW-ciz-um), which leaves them pale white, with almost no pigment whatsoever. The condition also occurs in species like snakes, birds, horses, and lions.

Because of their rarity and fish-fan demand, platinum arowanas can be worth huge sums of money. In 2007, Singapore-based fish breeders brought a platinum arowana to an aquarium exhibition. They turned down offers of around $50,000 for the fish, and eventually decided to keep it. Less famous platinum arowanas aren't quite as valuable, but can cost several thousand dollars each. That's a lot of cash, just to give your aquarium that "new fish smell."

## Pigments of Your Imagination

Leucistic animals are often mistaken for albinos, but there are differences. Albino creatures lack the pigment melanin, while those with leucism lack all pigment types. Albinos' eyes are pink, as red blood vessels show through in the absence of melanin. But leucistic animals have normal-colored eyes, because eye pigment is not affected by mutations causing leucism.

# Not for the Faint of Goat

M any animal species have a "fight or flight" response. When threatened, they attack (fight) or they run, fly, or slither away (flight). Some goats, however, have a third option: faint.

Myotonic goats, or "fainting goats," are a little smaller than most goats, and have big, slightly bulging eyes. Other than those traits, they look like your average four-legged, hairy-chinned, tin-can-eating billy or nanny goat. Until you startle them.

Fainting goats have a hereditary genetic condition called *myotonia congenita* (my-oh-TONE-ee-uh con-GEN-it-uh). Although the exact cause isn't known, the condition in other species (including humans) is caused by mutations in genes that code for cell membrane proteins. These mutations prevent tensed-up muscles from relaxing right away, as they normally would.

Despite the name, "fainting" goats don't actually faint when they're surprised. Instead, they tense up to run away, but all those tensed-up muscles freeze in place, and the goat can't run at all. Or walk, or stand. Startle a myotonic goat, and it'll usually stiffen up and keel over sideways. After a few seconds, its muscles will relax and the goat's as good as new.

Unless it was startled by something coming to eat it. That's where "faint" falls short of "fight" or "flight." Also, fainting goats miss the good parts of scary movies. It's a real problem.

## Nor Faint of People, Either

In people, more than 100 different mutations have been identified that cause myotonia congenita. Symptoms include stiff movements, joint problems, and—like the goats—falling during sudden movements. Sometimes, making repetitive movements can relieve symptoms, in a phenomenon called the "warm-up effect." Unfortunately, no one has mentioned this to the goats.

# My-Oh-Myostatin

Whippets are racing dogs descended from greyhounds. Over time, breeders noticed two unusual types of whippet puppies. Some dogs were extremely fast, even for whippets. Breeders liked these, so they often bred two "fast" whippets together, hoping for speedier pooches. The strategy worked, but it also produced a few dogs that were very different. These dogs, called "bully whippets," look like they've been working out at the gym, bulking up with "Arnold Shih-tzu-negger" or "Bark Lesnar." The dogs' muscles bulge out of their legs, chests, and backs. But why are these muscle-bound dogs found in the litters of "fast" whippet parents?

The answer lies in the myostatin (MY-oh-stat-in) gene. The protein coded by this gene regulates muscle development. When muscles are big enough, myostatin signals growth to stop.

Like most animal genes, there are two copies of myostatin in each cell. "Fast" whippets have a mutation that affects one copy of the gene. With a little less myostatin, these dogs only grow a little more muscle—enough to make their legs stronger and give them a racing edge.

But "bully" whippets inherit mutant myostatin genes from both parents, and can't make the protein at all. With no myostatin, their muscles bulge to nearly double the usual size. In fact, these whippets—who aren't really "bullies"; they're usually very sweet—can't race at all. They're too big. But they do impress everyone with their flexing down on "Muscle-mutt Beach."

Wendy, a bully whippet

# Whippets! Whippets Good!

Though whippets are smaller than their greyhound cousins, they run nearly as fast—up to 35 miles per hour—and accelerate faster than any breed. That includes greyhounds. Also Scooby Doo, being chased by a swamp monster. And all 101 Dalmatians. Whippets are seriously fast.

# Cat o' Nine ... Toes?

C at math must be really hard. Humans have built a lot of mathematics around the number 10, because all of us—or nearly all of us—have 10 fingers and toes to count with. As usual, though, cats are more complicated. Cats have 18 toes total—five on each front paw, and four on each back one. Except when they don't.

A fair percentage of cats are polydactyl (pol-ee-DACK-tull), meaning they have more toes than they really ought to. (Breaking it down, "poly" means "many" and "dactyl" means "finger" or "toe.") Polydactyl cats may have extra toes on one set of feet or on all four, up to eight little piggies per paw. The most toes on a single cat is 28, according to the *Guinness Book of World Records*. Those toes belong to a Canadian tabby named Jake, who may be able to count higher than most cats, but probably has trouble finding a decent pair of shoes.

Rather than a gene mutation, polydactyly is caused by a mutation in a region of DNA that regulates certain genes during development. When the region is mutated, a gene promoting toe formation on the embryo's paws gets activated where it shouldn't, and extra toes sprout out.

Cats aren't the only species with multiplying toes, though. Polydactyly also occurs in chickens, dogs, mice, and even humans. As if the metric system wasn't hard enough already.

One of the many polydactyl cats that lives on the Ernest Hemingway property.

## The Old Man and the C(-A-Ts)

Some famous polydactyl cats live in Key West, FL. The author Ernest Hemingway lived there, and was once given a polydactyl cat named Snow White. When Hemingway died in 1961, his cats were allowed to stay on the property. With the cats interbreeding over time, many of the nearly 50 now living there are polydactyl. Apparently, there hasn't been *A Farewell to Toes*.

# Bald Is Beautiful?

ome pets are man's best friend. Others are more like man's weird uncle, mostly because they desperately need a toupee. (They also make unpleasant noises at the dinner table, but scientists don't consider that a genetic mutation. Yet.) Most pooch and kitty fans love to snuggle next to a furry four-legged friend, but some dogs and cats are bred specifically for a genetic mutation that makes them bald.

Chinese crested dogs have an unusual look, with their bare skin and boy-band hair. These features are caused by genetic mutations, which make them quite a unique breed. Dogs usually pant to cool off, but Chinese crested dogs have sweat glands just like humans. Their genetic makeup can also cause them to have missing and crooked teeth. Between their ghastly grins and their bald bodies, the hairless Chinese crested has won more World's Ugliest Dog competitions than any other breed.

Don't worry, cat lovers. There's a bald mutant for you, too! The Sphynx cat has extremely fine hairs that make it appear completely bald. These hairs give their skin a suede-like texture, and their skin color can form common cat patterns, like calico or tabby.

The Chinese crested dog "Elwood" appears at the 2007 World's Ugliest Dog Contest.

## Not Quite a Sphynx

Despite its Egyptian name, the Sphynx cat breed started in Canada in 1966 from a single hairless mutant. Their large eyes and attentive ears give these cats a regal look, earning them the name Sphynx.

Siamese cat

# Mutant Trivia Answer

This popular pet has a color mutation that is sensitive to temperature. The animal will develop darker hair in colder areas of the body and lighter hair in warmer areas of the body. Who is this mutant?

a. A beagle
**b. A Siamese cat (correct)**
c. A long-haired guinea pig

The Siamese cat has a gene mutation that causes point coloration. Colder areas of the body, like the feet, face, and tail, will have darker hair than warmer areas of the body, like the torso. Point coloration also occurs in certain horses, sheep, and rabbits.

## Think About It

Bully whippets have a gene mutation that gives them super strength. If you had a pet, what super-mutant power would you want it to have? Get out your notebook or sketchpad and write a short story or draw a comic strip about you and your super-mutant pet on a dangerous superhero mission.

Australian redback
spider, a type of
widow spider

# 3 Mutants Underfoot

**From rats to spiders, there are plenty of critters** that scamper, scurry, and slither their way into our nightmares. None of the animals in this chapter need any help to give people a bad case of the willies, but they all have gene mutations that make them creepier, scarier, or deadlier.

## Do You Know Your Mutants?

A scientist kept a group of these critters in complete darkness for more than 50 years to study how their genes changed in extreme living conditions. What were they?

  a. Rats          b. Fruit flies          c. Black widow spiders

Find out the answer at the end of the chapter!

# A Really, REALLY Bad Hair Day

How do you do your hairdo? Are you a mousse-and-gel-er? A blowdry-and-brush-er? A wash-and-out-the-door-er? Hopefully, you're not a let-blood-sucking-bugs-crawl-on-your-head-er, but for those of us with luxurious locks, it's always a risk. Head lice are tiny wingless bugs that live in human hair and suck blood from your scalp. If that's not gross enough, these itchy insects have developed a genetic mutation that makes them resistant to lice-killing drugs, turning them into a real head-scratcher for doctors.

Lice are parasites, because they live at the expense of a host (meaning, you). They're like siblings who barge into your room uninvited, eat all your food, and borrow your stuff without asking. Head lice only affect humans, so you can't give them to—or get them from—your pets. (And Fido probably wouldn't be too disgusted if you did come home with a lice-covered skull. It's hard to gross out a critter that smells its own poop.)

A special insecticide medication usually kills them, but a population of "superlice" have popped up that are resistant to some of these drugs. These hair-wreckers are confirmed in 25 states already, and the actual numbers are probably higher. Fortunately, prescription medications can help treat these lice, so you don't have to split hairs with these notorious 'do-destroyers.

## The Name Is Bond, Lice Bond

Lice can't fly, hop, or teleport like Captain Kirk, so they can only get to your head by crawling. Once they find a delicious-looking noggin, they use special hook-like claws to climb up your hair like super spies and they set up their not-so-secret base on your scalp.

# The Lord of the Stings

Whether they're making you scream in a horror movie or just scaring the suds off you in the shower, spiders usually take the Number 1 spot on the Atrocious Arachnid list. Scorpions are probably a bit annoyed by this. With powerful pincers and a venomous whip-like tail, scorpions are both formidable foes and fearsome predators. Recently, a group of scientists compared scorpion and insect genes and found an answer to how scorpions developed their deadly sting.

Insects have a substance called *defensin* that protects them from bacteria, viruses, and other harmful germs. Scientists discovered that just one tiny gene mutation can turn certain insects' defensins into the scorpion venom. This suggests that these insects and scorpions evolved from a common ancestor, but a genetic mutation way back in the past turned these protective substances into deadly weapons for scorpions.

It takes a very brave (or very dumb) predator to grab a scorpion by its venom-filled tail, but scientists discovered that some species have a back-up line of defense—they can snap their tails off and run away. Unfortunately, this daredevil stunt leaves the scorpion with a pretty unsavory problem—it can't poop for the rest of its life. Despite this, these scorpions can continue to eat and can even mate for months. Just don't ever let these scorpions take the wheel on a long road trip. They're definitely *not* stopping at the next rest stop.

## A Pesticide With a Bite

Both spider and scorpion venoms have been tested as possible pesticides to protect crops. More recently, scientists used the venom of the funnel-web spider to create a pesticide that killed most insect pests, but did not harm honeybees, which farmers rely on to pollinate crops.

# One Predator's Poison Is Another's Brunch

L ife in the wild is a lot like a head-to-head duel in a video game. You pick a character who chucks ninja stars and your friend picks a character with a sword, and then you punch, kick, and combo your way to victory. (Unless your friend is winning. Then you "accidentally" hit the reset button and claim a power glitch, because the wild is also unfair.) Like video game characters, animals also have specialized defenses for the inevitable fight to the death.

Take the rough-skinned newt, for example. Its bright orange belly secretes an extremely potent toxin that kills almost anything that tries to swallow it. The newts try to warn predators of their poison first by showing them their bright orange underbelly. To do this, the newt arches his head toward his back feet. Scientists call it the *unkenreflex*. (It's an appropriate name. If we tried to bend our heads back to touch our feet, we'd be crying "unken!" too.) Often, this display convinces the predators to pass on the noxious newt, and they slither, scamper, or waddle on to rustle up some less toxic takeout.

Except for the garter snake. It has a gene mutation that makes it resistant to the newt's toxin. The newt can still try to trick it by flashing its "I'm poisonous!" belly, but if the snake calls its bluff, the newt's out of luck. Maybe the newts should look into a whole new weapon of defense. We're voting for ninja stars.

## GPS (Garter Positioning System)

Garter snakes don't need a GPS to get to another snake's home, because they can use their tongues to detect chemicals that other snakes leave. Even baby garter snakes can read these signals and follow chemical trails left by other snakes.

# Smelling a Rat Under the Microscope

Rats put up with a lot of guff from humans, given all the shrieking, jumping, and "Ew!"-ing we do when they scamper in front of us on the street. We detest them so much that we call untrustworthy people "dirty rats," we "rat someone out" to get them in trouble, and a messy school locker is considered a "rat's nest." Part of our fear is warranted, because rats can spread diseases. The most notorious case was the Black Death, a plague that killed millions of people in the 1300s.

The Black Death was named because the disease caused big black marks on the skin of infected people. Rats—and the fleas that lived on them—carried the plague bacteria, which transmitted to humans through bites. (Fleas can bite humans, not just pets.) People with the most serious infections died within days. But how did such tiny bacteria become so deadly?

Scientists recently studied the DNA of plague bacteria from people who died during the Black Death, and found that it developed two key gene mutations that turned it from a less harmful germ into a murderous microbe. Improved medical care and sanitation have decreased incidences of plague worldwide, but it's still a concern in some areas of the world. Understanding how it mutates can help scientists stay one step ahead of this "dirty rat" germ.

## Rat-Faced Burglars

Rats are masterminds of squeezing into human homes. They can push their bodies through very tiny spaces, and their teeth are strong enough to chew through lead. Their teeth never stop growing. Chewing through hard substances helps to grind their teeth down.

The rat flea played a major role in the spread of the bacterium that caused the Black Death of the Middle Ages.

41

Patella

Femur

Tibia

Metatarsus

Tarsus

# Knee Deep in
# Mutant Spiders

Nothing sends a chill up your spine faster than eight hairy legs scampering toward you (unless, of course, they are attached to two puppies). But if you're brave enough to look at a spider's legs, they are actually quite fascinating. Each leg has seven joints, which give them a lot of flexibility, but that's a lot of joints to coordinate just to move around.

Your kneecap bone is called the *patella*. Spiders do not have bones, but scientists use the word patella to describe the main "knee" joint that connects two sections of the spider's leg, the tibia and femur (which are also the names of the two large bones in your legs connected by your knee joint). Scientists recently discovered that spiders developed this patella from a duplication of the *dac* gene, short for the dachshund gene. (Yep, the gene that gave spiders "knees" is named after wiener dogs with short, stumpy legs.) When researchers deleted this double gene, the patella and tibia in spiders became one large leg segment. Without knees, these spiders walked stiffly, like little Frankenstein monsters. Well done, scientists. You managed to make spiders even creepier.

## Hydraulic Spiders

Spiders don't have complex muscle systems like humans do, so they flex their legs using hydraulics. Hydraulic engines are powered by the flow of pressurized fluid. Spiders have an open circulatory system, so their blood mixes with other fluids in their bodies. The pressure created by all of this fluid pushes the joint outward to flex. After death, this pressure releases, which is why spider legs curl up when they die.

Fruit fly

# Mutant Trivia Answer

A scientist kept a group of these critters in complete darkness for more than 50 years to study how their genes changed in extreme living conditions. What were they?

a. Rats
b. **Fruit flies (correct)**
c. Black widow spiders

In 1954, a Japanese scientist named Syuiti Mori put a group of fruit flies in a dark cave to see how the genes in the population would change over time. The flies stayed in the cave for more than 50 years, producing 1,400 generations of offspring. Although the changes to the fly were not as profound as expected, Syuiti's team did find mutations in a couple of key genes that may have increased the flies' survival in the dark, including one mutation that damaged the flies' natural light receptors.

## Think About It

Your favorite actor or actress calls you up. He or she wants to make a horror movie about a mutant critter, and they want you to write it. What creepy crawly will you pick? How will you mutate it? Draw your scariest movie poster for your mutant-a-rific masterpiece!

Cavendish
bananas

# 4 It Came . . . From the Garden!

**Plants seem pretty harmless. Some we eat. Some we sniff.**
Some need to get out of our way, because we keep walking into them when we're texting. (You hear that, big oak tree? We're talking to you.) Yet, there are quite a few amazing— if downright freaky—mutants that grow right out of our soil. Here are some of the weirdest that have sprouted up around us.

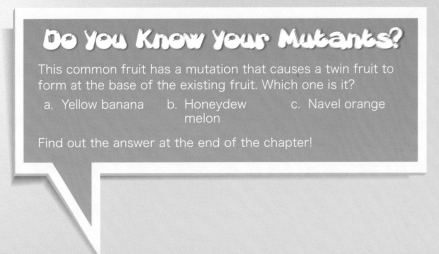

## Do You Know Your Mutants?

This common fruit has a mutation that causes a twin fruit to form at the base of the existing fruit. Which one is it?

a. Yellow banana    b. Honeydew melon    c. Navel orange

Find out the answer at the end of the chapter!

Teosinte

Modern corn

# Mutants of the Corn

D o you like popgrass? How about grassbread? Or grass pudding? A nice bowl of grassflakes? Unless you're a horse or sheep, probably not.

Replace "grass" with "corn," though, and there's a good chance you enjoy some of those foods. Worldwide, about 100 million metric tons of corn are eaten every year. But if not for a specific mutation, the corn we know would have never developed from the grass it used to be.

Corn, or maize, originally developed nearly 10,000 years ago from a wild grass plant called *teosinte* (tee-oh-SIN-tee). Species of teosinte still grow today—and they don't look much like corn. Instead of a single long stalk like corn, teosinte plants are bushy. The "ears" they produce are tiny compared to ears of corn, and only contain a few kernels. Worst of all (if you're a hungry corn-eater), each teosinte kernel is locked inside a hard outer shell, like a walnut.

The "hard shell" bit was the big problem with teosinte, and the place where corn got its start. Thanks to a single mutation in a gene called *tga1*, the shells on some plants didn't grow as well, and the kernels were exposed. Over time—and with some help from human farmers—the ears grew larger, with more kernels, into the familiar corn we know today.

Good thing, too. Who wants to eat "grass dogs" on a stick at the county fair? Blech.

## Corn-tinually Improving

Early farmers influenced the development of corn and other crops through a process called *selective breeding*. Each year, farmers would plant seeds from the "best" plants that grew the season before—the corn, for instance, with the biggest ears and most kernels. Over time, these desirable traits became more common and stronger throughout the crop population.

# Attack of the CLAVATA Tomatoes

**B**eefsteak tomatoes look like mutants. Misshapen, lumpy, and much bigger than normal, they can weigh a pound or more. They're like the Quasimodos of tomatoes. Quasimatoes.

Although beefsteak tomatoes have been around since at least the 1500s, no one knew why they grew that way—until 2015, when scientists looked at a different set of weird tomatoes. These plants grew more flowers and fruit than usual, which the researchers traced back to mutations affecting the behavior of CLAVATA proteins. In plants, proteins encoded by CLAVATA genes act within stem cells to slow growth during development. These proteins balance the growth process, so the plant doesn't grow too large for the food and energy available.

When the CLAVATA proteins are disrupted, though, growth goes all higgledy-piggledy. In the mutants the scientists began studying, this meant more flowers and fruit per plant. But when they looked at the genes of other tomatoes, they found a similar mutation in a particular gene, CLAVATA3, that leads to bigger, brawnier, bulbous tomatoes. Like the beefsteaks.

Because CLAVATA genes are in all plants, we might someday be able to fine-tune them to grow all sorts of bigger crops. So keep an eye out for beefsteak beets, beefsteak blueberries, or maybe even beefsteak broccoli. Now there's a veggie even Quasimodo would be afraid of.

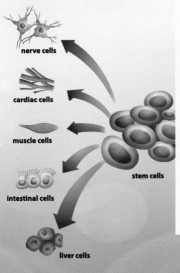

nerve cells

cardiac cells

muscle cells

intestinal cells

stem cells

liver cells

# The Secret Life of Stem Cells

Stem cells are cells in all plants and animals—including humans—that don't know what they want to be when they "grow up." Whereas a skin cell can only produce more skin cells or a hair cell more hair cells, stem cells can develop into many different types of cells—or into more stem cells. So they're very important during development and throughout an organism's life.

# Growing Little
# Green Aliens

T here are a lot of weird things happening in space, but our scientists from Earth can outweird most of them. For example, orbiting above your head right at this moment, there is a good chance that astronauts are hard at work pruning, watering, and tending a lush, green space garden that's growing right on the International Space Station (ISS).

The phrase *orbiting vegetable garden* sounds like a group of giggly scientists had *way* too much fun playing Mad Libs, but it's quite a serious mission. NASA wants to send a manned mission to Mars in the not-so-distant future, but it takes about 8 months to get there and there aren't exactly any drive-thru restaurants along the way. For humans to survive the trip, they need to be able to grow their food in the harsh conditions of space. That's where the space garden comes in.

Environmental changes—like plucking a plant from Earth and shooting it into space—can cause gene mutations to develop in the plants, and some of these mutations may hurt their ability to produce food for astronauts. The scientists also look for any mutations that improve plants' ability to survive in space, so they can genetically engineer plants with those mutations for long space voyages. This will keep the crew well-fed during their long road trip, and no astronauts will ever have an excuse to disobey their parents' wishes to eat their fruits and veggies.

## Not-So-Fast Food

In 2015, ISS astronauts sampled the veggies grown in the space garden. Before they could chow down, the first crops were sent down to Earth and tested for safety. We're guessing astronauts don't complain when their pizza delivery takes longer than 30 minutes.

# The Explosive-Eating Weed

T he chemical trinitrotoluene (TRY-nigh-tro-TALL-you-een)—also known as TNT—is a dangerous but useful explosive. The problem is, even after it's used (for mining, demolition, or by the military), TNT is still dangerous. Traces of TNT remain after explosions, which can kill plant life and cause cancer in animals nearby. How can we fight the dangers of TNT? With flowers, of course. Mutant flowers.

Scientists grew the flowering plant *Arabidopsis* (uh-rab-uh-DOP-sis) in soil with traces of TNT. They looked for plants that managed to grow there, then studied their genes to see what changes had occurred to help the plants survive. Plants with mutations in the gene MDHAR6 were resistant to TNT contamination, but even better, could help to clean TNT out of the soil.

That's because the protein coded by the MDHAR6 gene is part of what makes TNT dangerous to plants. The protein breaks TNT down into a form that's toxic and can eventually kill the plant. Without the MDHAR6 protein, the TNT was simply absorbed and stored by the *Arabidopsis* in cell walls—hard, rigid structures around the plants' cells.

This MDHAR6 mutation is a triple-whammy of TNT cleanup. First, mutant plants don't die themselves. Second, those plants pull TNT out of soil, so there's less of it polluting the area. And third, animals can't digest cell walls—if they eat mutant plants containing TNT, it passes right through. So even if flowers can't prevent explosions, they can still clean up the mess. Nice.

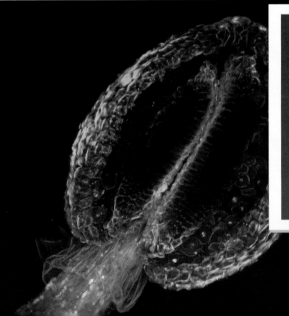

## That's One Popular Plant!

*Arabidopsis* (specifically, one species of *Arabidopsis* called *Arabidopsis thaliana*, or the less tongue-tying "mouse-ear cress") is the most widely studied plant in the world. It was the first plant to have its full genome sequenced and is used as a model for many plant genetics studies.

# Deadwood?
# Nope, It's a Redwood

I magine taking a long, relaxing stroll amongst the magnificent redwood trees in California. These trees reach heights of 370 feet tall—bigger than two Niagara Falls stacked on top of each other—and they can live thousands of years.

As you eye these jolly green giants, you may stumble across a rather odd sight: a redwood with pure white leaves. Many travelers call them ghost trees, but these forest spooks are not dead at all. They are albino redwoods. A gene mutation causes them to have a lack of chlorophyll, the green pigment that allows plants to photosynthesize. Unlike other green plants, these ghoulish-looking trees cannot make their own energy from the sun, so they become parasites, growing off other redwoods and sucking energy from them.

Because these trees are professional food moochers, they don't grow as large as other redwoods, but some of the tallest still reach heights of 70 feet. Redwoods are the only cone-producing trees known to have the albino mutation, and they are a quite rare sight. There are only a few albino trees known in the world, and a good percentage are found right in California. Now that's a Holly(red)wood ending, if we ever saw one.

## Duet of Me

Your DNA is your body's instruction manual to everything that makes up your body. But what if you had more than one manual? Chimeras have two or more sets of DNA, usually because two fertilized eggs fused together to make a single organism. Albino redwood chimeras have a mix of green and white leaves, and they are even rarer than other albino trees. Only 10 of these trees are known to exist in the world.

Looks like a belly button, but it's actually a second navel orange.

# Mutant Trivia Answer

This common fruit has a mutation that causes a twin fruit to form at the base of the existing fruit. Which one is it?

a. Yellow banana

b. Honeydew melon

c. **Navel orange (correct)**

When you break open a navel orange, those small orange pieces at the bottom are actually a second, underdeveloped "twin" fruit.

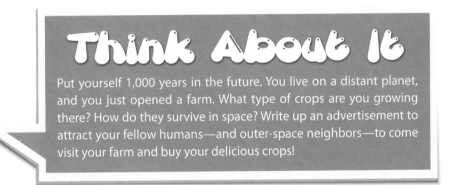

# Think About It

Put yourself 1,000 years in the future. You live on a distant planet, and you just opened a farm. What type of crops are you growing there? How do they survive in space? Write up an advertisement to attract your fellow humans—and outer-space neighbors—to come visit your farm and buy your delicious crops!

Red salamander

# 5 Color Me Mutated

**You can't always spot a mutant just by looking at it, but** organisms with color mutations definitely stand out from the crowd. From red to purple, two-toned to no-toned, mutants come in every color of the rainbow. Here are a few of the weirdest and freakiest ones out there.

## Do You Know Your Mutants?

Albinism is a gene mutation characterized by a lack of pigment in the skin and eyes. Which animal is most likely an albino?

a. A red salamander

b. A pink dolphin

c. An all-black zebra

Find out the answer at the end of the chapter!

# The Fiery Rocks of Mouse-dor

L ife in the wild is often a big game of hide-and-seek. The prey are the hiders, blending into the background and hoping they don't get caught. The predators are the seekers. Then someone screws the whole game up, because they need to go to the bathroom. (That may only happen to humans. There's probably no mid-hunt potty break in the wild.)

For prey animals, a good camouflage protects them from being spotted by predators. Take the rock pocket mouse. This tan-colored rodent blends into the deserts in the American Southwest, but the landscape is not completely sand-colored. Millions of years ago, volcanic eruptions poured lava into the area, which hardened into dark black rocks. Rock pocket mice also live around these rocks, except these mice are all black.

The black and tan rock pocket mice are the same species, but the black mouse has a gene mutation that gives it all-black fur. Against the sand, black mice would be spotted quite easily by predators, so any dark mice born there usually don't survive for very long. Around the black rocks, however, the darker mice camouflage better than their sandy-colored peers, proving that only the genetically chosen can survive amongst the fiery volcanic rocks of Mouse-dor.

## Neither Man nor Mouse

Despite their name, rock pocket mice are not true mice. They are rodents, but they are more closely related to gophers than to their squeaky namesakes. A rock pocket mouse's fluffy tail is longer than the critter's head and body combined and is used to maintain balance.

# On Hopperdays, We Wear Pink

**W**hen it comes to fashion, you can either choose to blend into the crowd or turn heads. Grasshoppers have the same quandary. Although many have a green or brown color to camouflage from predators, there is always that fashion-forward grasshopper that leaves its home decked head-to-wing in hot pink.

Hot pink grasshoppers don't choose to be fashionistas. Their coloring is most likely caused by a gene mutation that causes *erythrism* (ih-RITH-rizz-um), in which the organism produces an unusual amount of red pigment. If you happen to spot an adult pink grasshopper in the wild, you're quite lucky indeed. Many do not survive long enough to make it to adulthood, because their bright pink color makes them an easy-to-find meal for predators.

Erythrism exists in other animals, including raccoons, salamanders, and coyotes, but it's not common. And it may occur in even more species than we think. In 2013, a photographer in South Africa snapped a picture of a leopard with a pink tint to its coat, which people now call the Pink Panther. It's not known what precisely caused its unique coloring, but erythrism is one possibility.

## Color Me Toxic

Some species of grasshopper have bright colors to warn predators. Multicolored African variegated grasshoppers feed on poisonous plants and store chemicals from the plants in their bodies. Their bright, multicolored bodies warn predators that they are packed with deadly toxin.

# Come to the Dark (Meat) Side

I magine ordering a nice, juicy chicken dinner in a restaurant. Your mouth starts to water as soon as you see the waiter carrying the plate to the table, but when he plops it in front of you, the meat and bones are pitch black. What happened? Was it overcooked? Did the meat rot? Are you eating Darth Chicken? (We can't rule out that last one. Scientists don't know which side of the Force chickens fall on.)

If your chef cooked you an Ayam Cemani chicken, there is nothing wrong with your meal. Originally bred in Indonesia, these chickens have a genetic mutation known as *fibromelanosis* (FIE-bro-MEL-an-oh-sis). Melanin gives color to chicken feathers, skin, eyes, and other body parts. For chickens with fibromelanosis, their bodies are a little like putting a colored sock in a washing machine with all white clothes. The pigment travels everywhere, which is why almost every part of these chickens—feathers, skin, muscles, bones, and most internal organs—is completely black.

If you think their goth color makes Ayam Cemani chickens undesirable, think again. Farmers call them the Lamborghini chicken, after the sleek sports car brand. If you want one as a pet, be sure to cough up a hefty price for one. Due to their rarity in the United States, one Ayam Cemani chicken can sell for thousands of dollars.

## Staying in the Black

Some cultures believe that all-black chickens have medicinal properties. The Kadaknath chicken of India, another all-black chicken, is believed to bring vigor and good health to anyone who eats it.

# Piebaldism:
## When Some Little Pigments Stay Home

Commerson's dolphins, also referred to as piebald dolphins

I f you were painting a fence, you'd want to do a good job. That means covering all of it evenly with paint, and not leaving any colorless spots. If Tom Sawyer were painting a fence, he'd get someone else to do all the work, take a nap, and the job probably wouldn't get done very well. That fence might have irregular splotches of paint, with bare spots willy-nilly throughout.

In other words, the fence might look piebald. Piebaldism is a genetic disorder in humans and other animals that creates the same look as that half-painted fence. The condition is often caused by a mutation in the gene KIT, or the gene SNAI2. Some areas of the body are colored, usually black or brown, and others are white, with no color at all. The specific patterns are unpredictable, with islands of color and white appearing all over.

Piebaldism is a hereditary condition, which means it's passed down from mothers and fathers to their children. In addition to white patches of skin, piebald mammals also lose color in their hair, while birds lose feather coloring, and some snakes and fish grow white, colorless scales. But the exact coloration is distinct to each individual; even identical twins inheriting the same genetic mutation from their parents would develop different patterns of color and white.

Just like every Tom Sawyer-painted fence looks different. But never quite finished.

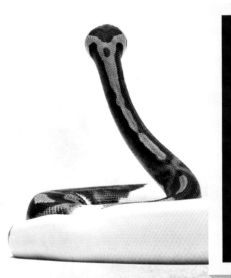

# Passing Down the Piebald

Our cells contain two copies of every gene, one inherited from our mother and the other from our father. Piebaldism is a "dominant" trait, which means if one of those copies—from mother or father—has the right mutation, the individual will be piebald. Other traits, like sickle cell anemia, are "recessive," meaning both copies must be mutated before the effect is seen.

# Pass the Pepper, Hold the Salt

A flock of black moths in a horror movie symbolizes doom and gloom, but for one little moth, rocking an all-black wardrobe actually helps it to survive. Found in temperate climates, the peppered moth is true to its name. Its white coloring peppered with black spots gives it a near-perfect camouflage from predators as it rests amongst the white lichens that grow on tree bark. Or it did, before humans screwed it up.

In the 1800s, the Industrial Revolution was in full swing. Big machines performed work that was once done by hand, factories sprouted up left and right, and cities grew larger. In industrialized areas where peppered moths lived, black soot from factories coated the trees and killed the lichens, making the white moths easy targets for predators. But a few moths had no problem surviving in this soot-filled environment, because they carried a gene mutation that made them almost completely black. Against light-colored lichens, their coloring would make them easy pickings for predators, but against the blackened trees, their color was an advantage. Over time, most of the moths found in industrialized areas were black.

In recent decades, improved pollution standards and cleaner fuel sources have allowed lichens to return, so the classic white peppered moth has made a big comeback in some regions. And that's the truth about the wild—sometimes it really is black and white.

## Just Wanna Have Fun(gi)

Lichens look like moss, but they are actually a combination of two organisms—fungi and algae. The algae create energy through photosynthesis, which feeds the fungus, and the fungus provides a moist, protected environment for the algae to grow.

# Mutant Trivia Answer

Albinism is a gene mutation characterized by a lack of pigment in the skin and eyes. Which animal is most likely an albino?

   a.   A red salamander

   **b.   A pink dolphin (correct)**

   c.   An all-black zebra

Although rare, albino dolphins do exist, and their skin is often colored pink, just like cotton candy. Between 2007 and 2015, an albino bottlenose dolphin named Pinky was spotted twice in the Calcasieu River ship channel in Louisiana.

# Think About It

Come up with a video game starring one of the color mutants in this chapter (or one that you research on your own). What is the goal of your game? How does the animal's color help or hurt it? Who or what are the villains?

Pink dolphin

73

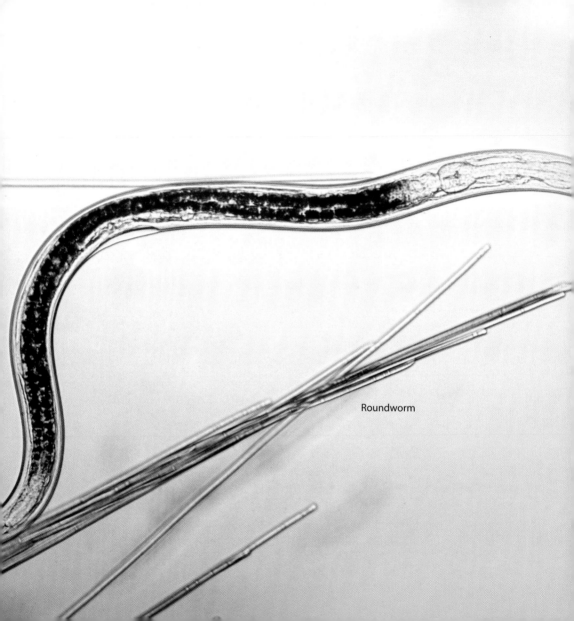

Roundworm

# 6 Weird and Engineered

**Many mutants born naturally in the wild are enough** to make us stop and point, but the wackiest genetic oddities come from the laboratory. Through genetic engineering, scientists can cut, pluck, and plop genes in and out of an organism's genome to make some pretty incredible critters. Here are a few of the cool mutants that popped out of the lab.

## Do You Know Your Mutants?

Scientists sometimes give goofy names to their lab mutants. This common research animal is named Casanova when it is born with a gene mutation that gives it two hearts. What is it?

a. White rat          b. Zebrafish          c. Nematode worm

Find out the answer at the end of the chapter!

# Lend Me Your Mouse Ears

**W**ith all their squeaking, mice are pretty noisy. In one laboratory, though, they're noisy *and* off-key. In Japan, a group of scientists has 100 singing mice. That's enough for a few seasons of Ameri-mouse Idol, or 25 barbermouse quartets.

The scientists wanted to know how gene mutations affected traits in future generations, so they mated mice that had a high risk of developing mutations in their genes. Imagine their surprise when one of the offspring started tweeting like a bird! The scien-

## Quiet as a Singing Mouse

Some mice are actually born to sing. In Costa Rica, two species of mice chirp like birds to attract mates and to mark their territory. When they sing, they get up on their hind legs, bend their heads back, and belt out their song. With such a knack for performance, you may one day see them headlining a Broadway show (probably *The Vermin of the Opera* or *Les Mouserables*).

tists bred their rat-tailed karaoke star, and now they have a lab full of singing mice (and plenty of earplugs, we hope). They hope the singing mice might give them a clue as to how humans developed speech.

Speaking of, there are speech-enhanced mice, too. A different group of scientists put human speech genes into mice and found that they formed a more complex range of "squeaks" to communicate with each other. Another study showed that mice with speech genes had a greater ability to learn by repetition (learning something by doing it over and over again), which may help us to understand how humans learn and retain words. It's still up in the air, but more research will hopefully help us to understand exactly why humans speak and mice squeak.

# When Flat Hair Is the Least of Your Worries

N o one wants to be flat. You don't want one of your jokes to fall flat, be flat out of something you need, or fall flat on your face. Our bodies are born to be magnificently un-flat, and a group of genetic engineers may have found one of the keys to our three-dimensional existence.

Being un-flat, especially given the fact that gravity pulls us toward the center of the Earth. If our bodies didn't have some way to resist this pull, we'd be flat puddle-like creatures sloshing around on the sidewalk. For humans and other vertebrates (organisms with backbones), the YAP gene allows our tissues to stick together and maintains the 3D shape of our organs.

Researchers mutated this gene in Japanese rice fish, and sure enough, the fish embryos could not maintain their organ shapes and their tissues flattened in the direction of gravitational pull. The researchers tried a similar experiment with human cells and found that the cells could not attach together properly to form tissues.

Basically, without YAP, we'd be flat out of luck.

## Defying Gravity

If you traveled to a planet with stronger gravity than Earth's, you'd need to wear a special suit to protect you from the crushing gravitational force. This is not true for any bacterial stowaways on your ship. A group of scientists discovered that bacteria can grow and reproduce normally under gravity that is 400,000 times stronger than Earth's.

# Eight- (and Four- and No-)
# Legged Freaks

I f you've ever walked into a spider web, you've noticed that spider silk is pretty strong stuff. (Or perhaps you were too busy shrieking to notice much of anything. We don't judge.) A super-thin strand of silk can dangle a much larger spider, and scientists think this silk could be used to make stronger surgical sutures, tougher body armor, and artificial body tissues. Unfortunately, spiders do not produce a ton of silk, so scientists came up with spider-worms.

Silkworms—the larvae of silkworm moths—use silk to make their cocoons. They make a lot more silk than your average spider, and the textile industry still uses them to make silk fabrics. Some crafty genetic engineers decided to get the best of both worlds by putting silk genes from spiders into silkworms. Although the silk these worms produce is not pure spider silk, it is about 50% stronger than the silk produced by an ordinary silkworm.

If spider worms aren't weird enough for you, there are also spider goats. The spider genes make the goats produce a large amount of spider-like silk in their milk, which may help scientists eventually learn how to produce enough spider silk for human use. If that doesn't work out, they could always test-drive a new superhero—SpiderGoatMan.

## Ten-Legged Freaks?

High on the list of Things No One Wants to See Scampering Across Their Bedroom Ceiling, scientists recently learned that manipulating certain spider genes can create 10-legged spiders. Learning how spiders' legs can mutate will help them better understand how spiders evolved to have eight legs in the first place.

# A Big Problem Needs a Pig Solution

There's a problem with pig poop.

Actually, there are several problems with pig poop, beginning with the smell. But one problem affects the environment in an unusual way. Like all organisms, pigs need the element phosphorus to live. On farms, pigs are fed grain containing phosphorus, but more than half is in a form the pigs can't digest. So most of it slides right through and comes out in the pigs' waste.

This phosphorus can then contaminate nearby lakes and ponds. Some algae species thrive on phosphorus and grow out of control, reducing oxygen levels and killing fish and other life.

One fix is to pull the phosphorus out of the pig poop before it can disrupt the environment. Because nobody wants to do that directly—again, the smell—scientists have found a way to genetically engineer pigs to reduce the phosphorus output. Better yet, it helps the pigs.

The key is a gene found in bacteria that produces a protein called *phytase* (FIE-tays), which breaks down the hard-to-digest form of phosphorus. When that gene is inserted into a pig's genome, the pig digests more of the phosphorus in the feed. Which means more phosphorus for the pig to use, and far less in the waste products. Happier pigs, a healthier environment, and improved pig poop. Now if only they could do something about the smell.

## Fed Up With Phytase?

Some farms solve the phosphorus pig poop problem without genetic engineering, by mixing phytase protein directly in the pigs' feed. Once eaten and in the pigs' digestive system, the phytase protein can break down phosphorus, just as before. But adding phytase to feed can be expensive and must be treated carefully before it's given to pigs or it may not function properly.

# Let There Be

# . . . Mutants!

Bioluminescent
mushrooms

**M**any creatures can produce light through chemical processes inside their bodies. These organisms—which include insect, bacteria, fungus, and jellyfish species, among others—are said to be "bioluminescent" (where "bio-" means "living" and "luminescent" means "glowing" or "light"). Some light up to signal danger or find a mate, while others glow steadily in the dark.

But why should those critters have all the fun? Scientists have identified many of the genes that allow bioluminescent species to light their own way and have inserted some of those genes into other plants and animals, allowing them to glow. Why? For science!

One common use for bioluminescent genes is to include them along with other genes engineered into an organism—like a gene providing disease resistance, for instance. Here, the light-enabling genes act as "reporters"; if cells contain the bioluminescent genes and light up, then the other genes have likely been incorporated into the genome, too. This technique has been used in species including plants, fish, frogs, mice, rabbits, pigs, sheep, cats, monkeys, and more.

Not all bioluminescent engineering projects are strictly scientific, however. Glowing fish are available from pet stores in a rainbow of colors, and some people have discussed engineering trees with bioluminescent genes to replace street lights in cities. What a bright idea!

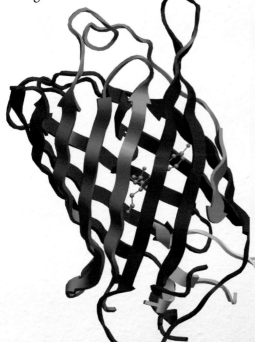

## Seeing Green

The bioluminescent gene most often used in genetic engineering originally comes from jellyfish. Called *green fluorescent protein*, or GFP, the protein encoded by the gene absorbs blue light and emits green light in response. In 2008, a team of scientists was awarded the Nobel Prize in chemistry for their discovery and early work with GFP.

Zebrafish

# Mutant Trivia Answer

Scientists sometimes give goofy names to their lab mutants. This common research animal is named Casanova when it is born with a gene mutation that gives it two hearts.

a. White rat

**b. Zebrafish (correct)**

c. Nematode worm

Researchers love to use zebrafish to study genes, because they are vertebrates (like humans) and they have transparent embryos, which are easy to study. Mutant zebrafish have plenty of goofy names, including Spock (born with pointed ears) and Dracula (born with a mutation that makes them sensitive to light).

## Think About It

Humans have always looked to nature to develop some of our best inventions. We make digging tools that look like animal claws and airplanes that look like magnificent birds. Think of your favorite plant or animal. What invention would you make that's inspired by its traits or behaviors? How would your invention benefit humankind?

Blue lobster

# Bibliography

## Introduction

Eveleth, R. (2013). *There are 37.2 trillion cells in your body. Smithsonian.com.* Retrieved from http://www.smithsonianmag.com/smart-news/there-are-372-trillion-cells-in-your-body-4941473

## Chapter 1
### Sea Monsters

ABC News. (n.d.). *Blind cave fish can grow eyes.* Retrieved from http://abcnews.go.com/Technology/story?id=120075

Ahmed, S. (2008). World's first six-legged octopus discovered. *CNN.* Retrieved from http://www.cnn.com/2008/TECH/03/04/octopus.uk

Antarctic Fish Biology. (n.d.). *Icefish.* Retrieved from https://sites.google.com/a/alaska.edu/antarctic-fish-biology/home/ice-fish

Aquarium of the Pacific. (n.d.). *Cone snails general description.* Retrieved from http://www.aquariumofpacific.org/onlinelearningcenter/species/cone_snails_general_description

Chivers, T. (2008). A hexapus, not a six-legged octopus. *The Telegraph*. Retrieved from http://www.telegraph.co.uk/news/uknews/1580533/A-hexapus-not-a-six-legged-octopus.html

Cossins, D. (2013). "White-blooded" icefish, 1927. *The Scientist*. Retrieved from http://www.the-scientist.com/?articles.view/articleNo/34797/title/-White-Blooded-Icefish-1927

de Pastino, B. (2006). Photo in the news: Lobster caught "half cooked" in Maine. *National Geographic*. Retrieved from http://news.nationalgeographic.com/news/2006/07/060720-lobster-photo.html

Erickson, J. (2012). Slow snails, fast genes: Predatory snails refine venoms through continuous gene duplication. *University of Michigan News*. Retrieved from http://ns.umich.edu/new/releases/20305-slow-snails-fast-genes-predatory-snails-refine-venoms-through-continuous-gene-duplication

Handwerk, B. (2008). Blind cavefish can produce sighted offspring. *National Geographic*. Retrieved from http://news.nationalgeographic.com/news/2008/01/080108-cave-fish.html

Jeffery, W. (2003). To see or not to see: Evolution of eye degeneration in Mexican blind cavefish. *Integrative and Comparative Biology, 43,* 531–541.

Kiger, P. J. (2015). New 'intraterrestrial' virus found in ocean depths. *Discovery News*. Retrieved from http://news.discovery.com/earth/oceans/new-intra terrestrial-virus-found-in-ocean-depths-150331.htm

Medrano, K. (2012). Odd-colored lobsters decoded. *National Geographic*. Retrieved from http://voices.nationalgeographic.com/2012/07/10/weird-wild-odd-colored-lobsters-decoded

National Geographic. (n.d.). *World's weirdest: Killer cone snail*. Retrieved from http://video.nationalgeographic.com/video/weirdest-cone-snail

New England Aquarium. (2013). *The colorful chemistry of lobster shells*. Retrieved from http://news.neaq.org/2013/08/the-colorful-chemistry-of-lobster-shells.html

Nosowitz, D. (2013). This weird fish has clear blood. *Popular Science*. Retrieved from http://www.popsci.com/science/article/2013-04/weird-fish-has-clear-blood

Owen, J. (2015). How this cave-dwelling fish lost its eyes to evolution. *National Geographic.* Retrieved from http://news.nationalgeographic.com/2015/09/150911-blind-cavefish-animals-science-vision-evolution

Paul, B., Bagby, S., Czornyj, E., Arambula, D., Handa, S., Sczyrba, A.,... Valentine, D. L. (2015). Targeted diversity generation by intraterrestrial archaea and archaeal viruses. *Nature Communications, 6,* 65–85.

Pittsburgh Zoo. (n.d.). *Blind cavefish.* Retrieved from http://www.pittsburghzoo.org/ppganimal.aspx?id=123

Safavi-Hemami, H., Gajewiak, J., Karanth, S., Robinson, S., Ueberheide, B., & Douglass, A., . . . Olivera, B. M. (2015). Specialized insulin is used for chemical warfare by fish-hunting cone snails. *Proceedings of the National Academy of Sciences, 112,* 1743–1748.

University of California-Santa Barbara. (2016). *The 'intraterrestrials': New viruses discovered in ocean depths.* Retrieved from http://www.sciencedaily.com/releases/2015/03/150323142843.htm

# Chapter 2

# Man's Freaky Best Friends

Arora, G., Mishra, S. K., Nautiyal, B., Pratap, S. O., Gupta, A., Beura, C. K., & Singh, D. P. (2011). Genetics of hyperpigmentation associated with the Fibromelanosis gene (Fm) and analysis of growth and meat quality traits in crosses of native Indian Kadaknath chickens and non-indigenous breeds. *Poultry Science, 52,* 675–685.

Beck, C., Fahlke, C., & George, A. (1996). Molecular basis for decreased muscle chloride conductance in the myotonic goat. *Proceedings of the National Academy of Sciences, 93,* 11248–11252.

Drögemüller, C., Karlsson, E. K., Hytonen, M. K., Perloski, M., Dolf, G., Sainio, K. . . . Leeb, T. (2008). A mutation in hairless dogs implicates FOXI3 in ectodermal development. *Science, 321,* 1462.

Eisenstadt, L. (2008). Hair of the dog. *Broad Institute.* Retrieved from http://www-genome.wi.mit.edu/news/1061

Gandolfi, B., Outerbridge, C., Beresford, L., Myers, J., Pimentel, M., & Alhaddad, H., . . . Lyons, L. A. (2010). The naked truth: Sphynx and Devon Rex cat breed mutations in KRT71. *Mammalian Genome, 21,* 509–515.

Lettice, L., Hill, A., Devenney, P., & Hill, R. (2007). Point mutations in a distant sonic hedgehog cis-regulator generate a variable regulatory output responsible for preaxial polydactyly. *Human Molecular Genetics, 17,* 978–985.

Mosher, D., Quignon, P., Bustamante, C., Sutter, N., Mellersh, C., Parker, H., & Ostrander, E. (2005). A mutation in the myostatin gene increases muscle mass and enhances racing performance in heterozygote dogs. *PLOS Genetics, 3*(5), e79.

PetMD. (n.d.). *4 fun facts about the Sphynx.* Retrieved from http://www.petmd.com/cat/pet_lover/MM_4funfacts_spynx

Shinomiya, A., Kayashima, Y., Kinoshita, K., Mizutani, M., Namikawa, T., Matsuda, Y., & Akiyama, T. (2011). Gene duplication of endothelin 3 is closely correlated with the hyperpigmentation of the internal organs (fibromelanosis) in silky chickens. *Genetics, 190,* 627–638.

Sutou, S. (2012). Hairless mutation: A driving force of humanization from a human-ape common ancestor by enforcing upright walking while holding a baby with both hands. *Genes to Cells, 17,* 264–272.

Uppsala Universitet. (2011). *Genetic study of black chickens shed light on mechanisms causing rapid evolution in domestic animals.* Retrieved from http://www.uu.se/en/news/news-document/?id=1567&typ=pm&area=2&lang=en

# Chapter 3
## Mutants Underfoot

American Lung Association. (n.d.). *Dust mites*. Retrieved from http://www.lung.org/our-initiatives/healthy-air/indoor/indoor-air-pollutants/dust-mites.html

American Museum of Natural History. (2014). *New findings: How do scorpions make their tails?* Retrieved from http://www.amnh.org/explore/news-blogs/research-posts/new-findings-how-do-scorpions-make-their-tails

Asthma and Allergy Foundation of America. (n.d.). *Dust mite allergy*. Retrieved from http://www.aafa.org/page/dust-mite-allergy.aspx

BioKids. (n.d.). *Common garter snake*. Retrieved from http://www.biokids.umich.edu/critters/Thamnophis_sirtalis

Blakemore, E. (2015). Lice that can resist drugs have infested half the states in the U.S. *Smithsonian.com*. Retrieved from http://www.smithsonianmag.com/science-nature/lice-can-resist-drugs-have-infested-half-states-us-180956308

Caspermeyer, J. (2015). Knee-deep in spider leg evolution. *Molecular Biology & Evolution, 33*(1), 296–297.

Centers for Disease Control and Prevention. (n.d.). *Parasites–Lice–Head lice*. Retrieved from http://www.cdc.gov/parasites/lice/head

Centers for Disease Control and Prevention. (n.d.). *Plague*. Retrieved from http://www.cdc.gov/plague/history

Coles, J. (2014). How the scorpion's venomous sting evolved. *BBC*. Retrieved from http://www.bbc.co.uk/nature/25683544

Connor, S. (1994). Scorpion's gene used to engineer pesticide: Venom introduced into virus kills caterpillars more quickly and highlights alternatives to chemicals. *The Independent*. Retrieved from http://www.independent.co.uk/

news/uk/scorpions-gene-used-to-engineer-pesticide-venom-introduced-into-virus-kills-caterpillars-more-1393514.html

DeMarco, E. (2015). How spiders got their knees. *Science*. Retrieved from http://www.sciencemag.org/news/2015/10/how-spiders-got-their-knees

Encyclopedia Britannica. (n.d.). *Plague*. Retrieved from http://www.britannica.com/science/plague

Erickson, J. (2014). Sharing that crowded holiday flight with countless hitchhiking dust mites. *University of Michigan News*. Retrieved from http://www.ns.umich.edu/new/releases/22564-sharing-that-crowded-holiday-flight-with-countless-hitchhiking-dust-mites

Fessenden, M. (2015). These two mutations turned not-so-deadly bacteria into the plague. *Smithsonian.com*. Retrieved from http://www.smithsonianmag.com/smart-news/these-two-mutations-turned-not-so-deadly-bacteria-mass-murdering-one-180955816

Hanifin, C. T., Brodie, E. D., III, & Brodie, E. D., Jr. (2003). Tetrodotoxin levels in eggs of the rough-skin newt, Taricha granulosa, are correlated with female toxicity. *Journal of Chemical Ecology, 29,* 1729–1739.

The Infinite Spider. (2014). *Spider legs and how they work*. Retrieved from http://infinitespider.com/spider-legs-work

Izutsu, M., Zhou, J., Sugiyama, Y., Nishimura, O., Aizu, T., Toyoda, A., . . . Fuse, N. (2012). Genome features of "dark-fly," a drosophila line reared long-term in a dark environment. *Plos ONE, 7*(3), e33288.

Mattoni, C., García-Hernández, S., Botero-Trujillo, R., Ochoa, J., Ojanguren-Affilastro, A., Pinto-da-Rocha, R., & Prendini, L. (2015). Scorpion sheds 'tail' to escape: consequences and implications of autotomy in scorpions (Buthidae: Ananteris). *Plos ONE, 10*(1), e0116639.

McKenna, P. (2016). Toxic newts lose war against 'super-immune' snakes. *New Scientist*. Retrieved from https://www.newscientist.com/article/dn13438-toxic-newts-lose-war-against-super-immune-snakes

Memorial Sloan Kettering Cancer Center. (2015). *Scorpion venom.* Retrieved from https://www.mskcc.org/cancer-care/integrative-medicine/herbs/scorpion-venom

Pearce, G., Yamaguchi, Y., Munske, G., & Ryan, C. A. (2008). Structure–activity studies of AtPep1, a plant peptide signal involved in the innate immune response. *Peptides, 29,* 2083–2089.

Phys.org. (2014). *How a scorpion gets its sting.* Retrieved from http://phys.org/news/2014-01-scorpion.html

Phys.org. (2015). *Knee-deep in spider leg evolution.* Retrieved from http://phys.org/news/2015-10-knee-deep-spider-leg-evolution.html

Rockney, H., & Wu, K. (2015). Rough-skinned newt. *Burke Museum.* Retrieved from http://webdev01v.burke.washington.edu/blog/rough-skinned-newt

Sun, X. (2015). History and current status of development and use of viral insecticides in China. *Viruses, 7,* 306–319.

Wisconsin Historical Society. (2006). *Lice comb from Fort Crawford.* Retrieved from http://www.wisconsinhistory.org/Content.aspx?dsNav=N:4294963828-4294963805&dsRecordDetails=R:CS2716

Yates, D. (2014). Of lice and men (and chimps): Study tracks pace of molecular evolution. *Illinois News Bureau.* Retrieved from https://news.illinois.edu/blog/view/6367/204678

Zielinski, S. (2015). Plague pandemic may have been driven by climate, not rats. *Smithsonian.com.* Retrieved from http://www.smithsonianmag.com/science-nature/plague-pandemic-may-have-been-driven-climate-not-rats-180954378

# Chapter 4

# It Came . . . From the Garden!

Blancaflor, E. (n.d.). *Advanced plant experiments 03-1.* Retrieved from http://www.nasa.gov/mission_pages/station/research/experiments/1062.html

Granath, B. (2013). *Experiment helping study plant growth in space.* Retrieved from http://www.nasa.gov/mission_pages/station/research/news/BRIC.html

Herkewitz, W. (2015). Scientists discover mutant plant that safely digests TNT. *Popular Mechanics.* Retrieved from http://www.popularmechanics.com/science/green-tech/a17203/mutant-plant-digests-tnt

Herridge, L. (2015). *Meals ready to eat: Expedition 44 crew members sample leafy greens grown on space station.* Retrieved from https://www.nasa.gov/mission_pages/station/research/news/meals_ready_to_eat

Humboldt Redwoods State Park. (n.d.). *Albino redwoods a winter treat.* Retrieved from http://redwoods.info/showrecord.asp?id=3257

Ibarra-Laclette, E., Lyons, E., Hernández-Guzmán, G., Pérez-Torres, C., Carretero-Paulet, L., & Chang, T., . . . Herrera-Estrella, L. (2013). Architecture and evolution of a minute plant genome. *Nature, 498,* 94–98.

Jaret, P. (2014). *Rare "albino" redwood may hold clues to the super-trees' longevity. National Geographic.* Retrieved from http://news.nationalgeographic.com/news/2014/03/140319-redwood-albino-chimera-california-tree-tallest

Johnston, E., Rylott, E., Beynon, E., Lorenz, A., Chechik, V., & Bruce, N. (2015). Monodehydroascorbate reductase mediates TNT toxicity in plants. *Science, 349,* 1072–1075.

Lee, R. (2015). Scientists pinpoint exact mutation that turned corn into a power crop. *Tech Times.* Retrieved from http://www.techtimes.com/articles/72707/20150729/scientists-pinpoint-exact-mutation-that-turned-corn-into-a-power-crop.htm

Leushkin, E., Sutormin, R., Nabieva, E., Penin, A., Kondrashov, A., & Logacheva, M. (2013). The miniature genome of a carnivorous plant Genlisea aurea contains a low number of genes and short non-coding sequences. *BMC Genomics, 14,* 476.

Ludwig-Maximilians-Universitat Munchen. (2014). *Plants with pocket-sized genomes.* Retrieved from https://www.en.uni-muenchen.de/news/newsarch iv/2014/heubl_botanik.html

NASA. (n.d.). *Humans to Mars.* Retrieved from http://www.nasa.gov/offices/ education/programs/national/dln/events/Humans_To_Mars.html

National Park Service. (n.d.). *About the trees.* Retrieved from http://www.nps. gov/redw/learn/nature/about-the-trees.htm

Rogers, K. (2015). Chimera. *Encyclopaedia Britannica.* Retrieved from http:// www.britannica.com/topic/chimera-genetics

Sayres, M. W. (2013). *Accessible research: A tiny bladderwort (that's a plant with little "bladders") genome.* Retrieved from http://pandasthumb.org/archives/ 2013/05/accessible-rese-1.html

Tarr, P. (2015). *Scientists pinpoint genes that make stem cells in plants, revealing origin of beefsteak tomatoes.* Retrieved from https://www.cshl.edu/news-and-features/scientists-pinpoint-genes-that-make-stem-cells-in-plants-reveal ing-origin-of-beefsteak-tomatoes.html

Thornton, S. (2011). *White wonders. National Geographic.* Retrieved from http:// education.nationalgeographic.org/news/white-wonders

Wang, H., Studer, A., Zhao, Q., Meeley, R., & Doebley, J. (2015). Evidence that the origin of naked kernels during maize domestication was caused by a single amino acid substitution in tga1. *Genetics, 200,* 965–974.

Welsh, J. (2010). A creepy monster of the forest: The albino, vampiric redwood tree. *Discover Magazine.* Retrieved from http://blogs.discovermagazine.com/ discoblog/2010/12/08/a-creepy-monster-of-the-forest-the-albino-vampiric-redwood-tree/#.Vqw2gTjlvIU

Xu, C., Liberatore, K. L., MacAlister, C. A., Huang, Z., Chu, Y. H., Jiang, K., . . . Lippman, Z. B. (2015). A cascade of arabinosyltransferases controls shoot meristem size in tomato. *Nature Genetics, 47,* 784–792.

# Chapter 5

# Color Me Mutated

Ainsworth, C. (2003). The stranger within. *New Scientist.* Retrieved from https://www.newscientist.com/article/mg18024215-100-the-stranger-within

Becker, R. A. (2015). How did rare pink dolphin get its color? *National Geographic.* Retrieved from http://news.nationalgeographic.com/2015/09/150909-pinky-albino-bottlenose-dolphin-animals-science

Bowen, R. (1998). *Mosaicism and chimerism.* Retrieved from http://www.vivo.colostate.edu/hbooks/genetics/medgen/chromo/mosaics.html

Damé, M., Xavier, G., Oliveira-Filho, J., Borges, A., Oliveira, H., Riet-Correa, F., & Schild, A. (2012). A nonsense mutation in the tyrosinase gene causes albinism in water buffalo. *BMC Genetics, 13*(1), 62.

Encyclopaedia Britannica. (2014). *Peppered moth.* Retrieved from http://www.britannica.com/animal/peppered-moth

Farkas, T., Mononen, T., Comeault, A., Hanski, I., & Nosil, P. (2013). Evolution of camouflage drives rapid ecological change in an insect community. *Current Biology, 23,* 1835–1843.

Genetics Home Reference. (n.d.). *Piebaldism.* Retrieved from http://ghr.nlm.nih.gov/condition/piebaldism

Hannam, S., & Rutowski, R. (n.d.). *The peppered moth: A seasoned survivor.* Retrieved from https://askabiologist.asu.edu/peppered-moth

Houston Museum of Natural Science. (2010). *A Valentine's Day surprise, a pink grasshopper!* Retrieved from http://blog.hmns.org/tag/erythrism

Howard Hughes Medical Institute. (2016). *Color variation over time in rock pocket mouse populations.* Retrieved from http://www.hhmi.org/biointeractive/color-variation-over-time-rock-pocket-mouse-populations

John P. Hussman Institute for Human Genomics. (2016). *Genetics basics lesson 3: Modes of inheritance.* Retrieved from http://hihg.med.miami.edu/code/http/modules/education/Design/Print.asp?CourseNum=1&LessonNum=3

Malakoff, D. (2014). Half-male, half-female bird has a rough life. *Science.* Retrieved from http://www.sciencemag.org/news/2014/12/half-male-half-female-bird-has-rough-life

The Mammals of Texas. (n.d.). *Rock pocket mouse.* Retrieved from http://www.nsrl.ttu.edu/tmot1/chaeinte.htm

McCusick, V. A., & Bocchini, C. A. (2012). *#172800: Piebald trait, PBT.* Retrieved from http://www.omim.org/entry/172800

Moore, J. D., & Ouellet, M. (2014). Review of colour phenotypes of the Eastern Red-backed Salamander, Plethodon cinereus, in North America. *Canadian Field Naturalist, 128,* 250–259.

Oetting, W., & King, R. (1999). Molecular basis of albinism: Mutations and polymorphisms of pigmentation genes associated with albinism. *Human Mutation, 13,* 99–115.

University of Utah Learn.Genetics. (n.d.). *Rock pocket mice.* Retrieved from http://learn.genetics.utah.edu/content/selection/comparative

U.S. Department of Agriculture. (n.d.). *What are lichens?* Retrieved from http://www.fs.fed.us/wildflowers/beauty/lichens/whatare.shtml

Wall, T. (2012). Fair-furred leopard is a true pink panther. *Discovery News.* Retrieved from http://news.discovery.com/animals/fair-furred-leopard-a-fashion-forward-feline-120413.htm

# Chapter 6

## Weird and Engineered

American Society of Animal Science. (2013). *Scientists improve transgenic 'Enviropigs.'* Retrieved from http://www.sciencedaily.com/releases/2013/03/130307124802.htm

BBC News. (2012). *The goats with spider genes and silk in their milk.* Retrieved from http://www.bbc.com/news/science-environment-16554357

Biello, D. (2011). Jellyfish genes make glow-in-the-dark cats. *Scientific American.* Retrieved from http://blogs.scientificamerican.com/observations/jellyfish-genes-make-glow-in-the-dark-cats

Braconnier, D. (2011). *Bacteria can grow under extreme gravity: Study.* Retrieved from http://phys.org/news/2011-04-bacteria-extreme-gravity.html

Discovery News. (2010). *'Singing mouse' made with genetic modification.* Retrieved from http://news.discovery.com/animals/zoo-animals/mouse-tweets-genetic-modification-101221.htm

Discovery News. (2013). *Genetically engineered silkworms spin like spiders.* Retrieved from http://news.discovery.com/tech/spider-silk-silkworms-genetic-engineering.htm

Fecht, S. (2012). 6 spider-silk superpowers. *Popular Mechanics.* Retrieved from http://www.popularmechanics.com/science/health/g741/6-spider-silk-superpowers/?slide=6

Food and Agriculture Organization of the United Nations. (n.d.). *Banana varieties resistant to fungus are identified using mutation induction.* Retrieved from http://www.fao.org/in-action/banana-varieties-resistant-to-fungus-are-identified-using-mutation-induction/en

Khadjeh, S., Turetzek, N., Pechmann, M., Schwager, E. E., Wimmer, E. A., Damen, W. G., & Prpic, N. M. (2016). Divergent role of the Hox gene Antennapedia in spiders is responsible for the convergent evolution of abdominal limb repression. *Proceedings of the National Academy of Sciences, 109,* 4921–4926.

Minard, A. (2010). Gene-altered "enviropig" to reduce dead zones? *National Geographic.* Retrieved from http://news.nationalgeographic.com/news/2010/03/100330-bacon-pigs-enviropig-dead-zones

Ordonez, N., Seidl, M., Waalwijk, C., Drenth, A., Kilian, A., Thomma, B. . . . Kema, G. H. J. (2015). Worse comes to worst: Bananas and Panama disease—When plant and pathogen clones meet. *PLOS Pathogens, 11*(11), e1005197.

Ossola, A. (2015). Researchers find the gene that makes us 3D. *Popular Science.* Retrieved from http://www.popsci.com/researchers-find-gene-makes-us-3d

Pasch, B., Bolker, B. M., & Phelps, S. M. (2013). Interspecific dominance via vocal interactions mediates altitudinal zonation in neotropical singing mice. *The American Naturalist, 182,* E161–E173.

Porazinski, S., Wang, H., Asaoka, Y., Behrndt, M., Miyamoto, T., Morita, H., . . . Furatani-Seiki, M. (2015). YAP is essential for tissue tension to ensure vertebrate 3D body shape. *Nature, 521,* 217–221.

Schreiweis, C., Bornschein, U., Burguière, E., Kerimoglu, C., Schreiter, S., Dannemann, M., . . . Graybiel, A. M. (2014). Humanized Foxp2 accelerates learning by enhancing transitions from declarative to procedural performance. *Proceedings of the National Academy of Sciences, 111,* 14253–14258.

Scientific American. (2006). *Why is spider silk so strong?* Retrieved from http://www.scientificamerican.com/article/why-is-spider-silk-so-str

Singer, E. (2009). Glowing monkeys inherit jellyfish genes. *MIT Technology Review.* Retrieved from https://www.technologyreview.com/s/413616/glowing-monkeys-inherit-jellyfish-genes

Suzuki, M. (2010). *Japan bio-scientists produce 'singing mouse.'* Retrieved from http://phys.org/news/2010-12-japan-bio-scientists-mouse.html

Than, K. (2011). Bacteria grow under 400,000 times Earth's gravity. *National Geographic.* Retrieved from http://news.nationalgeographic.com/news/2011/04/110425-gravity-extreme-bacteria-e-coli-alien-life-space-science

Moon Jellyfish

# About
# the Authors

Jenn and Charlie are Boston-based science nerds who met through stand-up comedy. By day, Jenn writes science textbooks and Charlie slings data for a cancer research company. By night, they make comedy films and stay up past their bedtime e-mailing pictures of weird animals to each other.

Albino Egyptian fruit bat

# Image Credits